YOUR KNOWLEDGE HAS VALUE

- We will publish your bachelor's and master's thesis, essays and papers

- Your own eBook and book - sold worldwide in all relevant shops

- Earn money with each sale

Upload your text at www.GRIN.com and publish for free

Bibliographic information published by the German National Library:

The German National Library lists this publication in the National Bibliography; detailed bibliographic data are available on the Internet at http://dnb.dnb.de .

Imprint:

Copyright © 2015 GRIN Verlag, Open Publishing GmbH
Print and binding: Books on Demand GmbH, Norderstedt Germany
ISBN: 978-3-668-07392-0

This book at GRIN:

http://www.grin.com/en/e-book/308941/modernity-and-tradition-in-chinua-achebe-s-girls-at-war-and-ngugi-wa

Ana María Leiva Aguilera

Modernity and Tradition in Chinua Achebe's "Girls at War" and Ngugi Wa Thiong'o's "A Meeting in the Dark"

GRIN Publishing

GRIN - Your knowledge has value

Since its foundation in 1998, GRIN has specialized in publishing academic texts by students, college teachers and other academics as e-book and printed book. The website www.grin.com is an ideal platform for presenting term papers, final papers, scientific essays, dissertations and specialist books.

Visit us on the internet:

http://www.grin.com/

http://www.facebook.com/grincom

http://www.twitter.com/grin_com

Modernity and Tradition in "Girls at War" and "A Meeting in the Dark".

Inhaltsverzeichnis

Introduction

The aim of this essay is to analyse two short African stories, each of them belonging to different areas. I will be focusing my attention on Chinua Achebe from Nigeria (West Africa) author of the short story "Girls at War" and Ngugi Wa Thiong'o 's "A Meeting in the Dark", from Kenya (East Africa).

Nonetheless, both short stories share an important contrast between modernity (as a result of European influence on the part of colonizers) and tradition (the combination of cultural and social features characterizing African people's identity). We have to make reference to Yeats in order to explain this contrast. According to Paula García in her doctoral thesis: *"El irlandés tenía un concepto cíclico de que la historia se sucede de forma destructiva"*[1] On the other hand, we should consider the concept of decolonization which took place during the 1950s and led path to a debate in the choice of language for writing literature. Language acts as another element which divides tradition (aboriginal languages) and modernity (language of the colonizer): Ngugui wa Thiong'o supported the unique use of African languages in literature but it was after he wrote this story, which was in English. He said that the language of the colonizer was a symbol of his identity, a way of accepting European culture. On the contrary, Achebe decided to write in English because he wanted to address to the whole nation by means of a central language. Even, he considered that the use of English opened him more opportunities for his message to be read throughout Europe. This Western cultural background and clash between European and original African identities gives as result the concept of cultural syncretism, which will be a key concept for this analysis. These short stories are a written literary proof of how African people found themselves in a constant fight for keeping their original believes and traditions, trying to achieve success through European literacy but never being accepted as fully Westernized nor as fully Africans anymore[2].

1García P. 1998, p.412.

2"A major feature of post-colonial literatures is the concern with place and displacement. It is here that the special post-colonial crisis of identity comes into being" (Ashcroft, B. 1989, p. 8)

Two opposing forces: Tradition vs Modernity

On the one hand, Chinua Achebe is an African author from Nigeria, West Africa. In "Girls at War", short story which appears in the collection *Girls at War and Other Stories* (1976) we find political subjects such as the struggle Africans faced for achieving Ibo's independence: "The war of Biafra" (1967-1970) is the main topic in this story, functioning as a perfect revelator of social distinctions as well as differences concerning gender: the only option a woman had for surviving in a war was by means of prostitution just like Gladys did (tradition). Achebe is revealing how corruptive power (modernity) may lead to destruction and injustice. We part from hope and move towards disillusionment little by little throughout this short story.

The story begins with a third person narrator introducing us the first time in which Reginald Nwankwo, an important official, and Gladys, a beautiful young woman, meet. Achebe looks for the preservation of proverbs of the Ibo community by means of this stories: "Somebody else shouted *"Irrevolu!" and his friends replied "shum!" "Irrevulu"*, *"shum", "Isofeli?" "Mba!"* (p. 157). So this use of Ibo language is a gesture towards the richness of Nigerian folktales: griots went from one village to another in order to tell stories just like literature passes from one hand to another in a more spread like travel than the one of griots. This is the power of literature as preservation and expansion of the Ibo tradition.

On the other side, the Red Cross was an association for fighting in the war supporting the Ibo independence and an essential indicative of progress towards revolution. People were being more and more instructed in schools since colonization and this immersion into opportunities of reading woke up in them a feeling of activation even in the female figure: "girls from a local secondary school marching behind a banner: WE ARE IMPREGNABLE!"

This fragment is taken from the early stages of the war in which Reginald Nwankwo has just left Owerri and meets a group of militia girls, among them was Gladys. This is an important evolution from the traditional African woman who stays at home, being submissive towards a more modern kind of woman revealing during the Biafran War.

Ibos wanted to be independent and these girls were rising up their voice which is a great movement from silence towards revelation, from tradition towards modernity.

In this phase, Nigeria's Civil War is the main theme, as above mentioned. Achebe was a direct witness and took the role of historian in the village, as a direct figure in the transmission of the new European influence to their people. The third time they meet, war left horrible consequences: *"Death and starvation, having long chased out the headiness of the early days, now left in some places blank resignation"* (.p 157). There is again a coming back towards tradition, girls are not so revolutionary now but will take advantage of their bodies in order to survive in the war: *"Girls became girls once more and boys boys". It was a tight, blockaded, and desperate world but nonetheless a world"* (p. 157). Gladys has changed, just like the war has: *"You've changed, Gladys. You were always beautiful, of course, but now you are a beauty queen. What do you do these days?"* (p. 158). We are seeing the depiction of a war through the figure of a woman: Gladys is in a crowd, he sees and takes her but she is not the same anymore, she is wearing a wig, make up and even expensive clothes. She is now the wife of a corrupt bureaucrat[3]. Reginald used to admire her because of her former capacity of revolution and remaining naïve at the same time. But now he knows that he only wants to sleep with her, as if she was an object. This symbol reminds us both to tradition as modernity: it is tradition because Achebe is expressing the selfish human nature, the savage one of covering necessities and at the same time, it may be a wink to modernity: Gladys has been influenced by the Westernized world. Even she has covered herself both metaphorically (she has sold her identity in order to survive) as literally (by wearing this artificial European make up and wig). The role of Gladys in this context is exactly that, the one of an object of desire: *"Don't be so scared, he said. She moved closer and he began to kiss her and squeeze her breasts"* (p. 162).

We have to bear in mind that this is also a story of survival and she has to take advantage of her body in order to remain alive. But this survive is in a sense mixed with

---

3 *"Gladys es un producto de la Nigeria postcolonial […] en un primer momento, ella gobierna su vida, aunque al final se ve inmersa por los acontecimientos propios de la guerra"* (García P. 1998, p. 416)

love because it seems that there have always been something magical in them, a series of encounters maybe arranged by destiny. They cannot help meeting and every time they do this, important changes have taken place. Their encounters are like hidden testimonies in the rearguard. In relation to these constant encounters on the part of destiny, there is a reference to tradition because Igbo people believed that there existed some kind of personal god which was like the lost part of every person. This reminds us to soul mates and how they would be encountered by means of destiny: *"the Igbo also believe in the existence of a personal god, or chi, which is a sort of spiritual double of each individual human"*[4].

Another issue dealing with tradition vs modernity is found in the fragment of the party in which a white European drunk pilot made a grotesque commentary addressing to the way women sold their bodies in order to survive in the war: *"Even these girls who come here[...] what are they worth? [...] a head of a stockfish [...] or one American dollar and they are ready to tumble into bed"* (p. 163). He was unconsciously making reference to one of the realities found in the war and it deeply made Reginald to agree with him but we will discover it later in page 165 after the party: *"He would stand up beside the fellow and tell the party that here was a man of truth. What a terrible fate to befall a whole generation!"* This makes reference to the traditional concept of community which is translated into a more "Modern" like context in which parties between people of power are a new way of being accepted by this community and thinking alike but never giving another perspective out aloud or you would be taken as an outcast and excluded.

The fact that a young black officer slapped the drunk white man made the women present in the party to see him as a hero: *"And all the girls showed with their eyes that they rated him a man and a hero"* (p. 163). This admiration of the male as a heroic epic figure reminds us to the traditional figure of men like protectors. Even, having a black man who wins the black man is a symbol of tradition (Black African hero) over modernity (white Europeans).

4Booker, K. 2003, p. 91

Nonetheless, this fact of the drunk man makes Reginald to ponder about Gladys as a mirror which represents part of a degrading, desperate for surviving war immersed society: *"Gladys, he thought, was just a mirror reflecting a society that had gone completely rotten and maggoty at the center"* [...] *"all that needed was a clean duster"*(p. 165). So at the end of the party, they slept together and *"He might just as well have slept with a prostitute, he thought"*. (p. 165).

At the end of the story, there is a moment of epiphany: Reginald Nwankwo who had been a corrupt by stealing food for the refugees in order to give it to their family, realizes about the real and problematic war situation thanks to the first image of an ambitious Gladys in the Red Cross, making an effort for Nigerian independence. So he decides to give her part of this food: this is a symbol of human beings' ability of empathy, which reminds us to Rousseau's theory of the "noble savage", which affirms that human beings are not so evil in nature but it is society, power and progress that make us become corrupt: "The term "noble savage" expresses the concept of the so-called "natural man," untouched by the supposedly corrupting influences of civilization. The term is founded on the belief that in a state of nature, human beings are essentially good" [5]This is not the only good action he does, but at the very end tries to help a wounded soldier. There is a feeling of solidarity which makes us think in traditional African tales in which a member of the tribe would help and treat another member as an equal against problems. These didactic tales Achebe bases on were told orally to the children of the tribe so that they acquired a set of values on their community. [6]

In the end, Nwankwo is unfulfilled because he loses what he tried to save. Everyone dies in an explosion in the war: *"He saw the remains of his car smoking and the entangled remain of the girl and the soldier"*. (p. 168). Modernity leads to corruption and this is especially frequent in tense situations like wars. This conflict was not only a conflict between the Ibos and the Federal Government: Europeans ended by supporting Nigerian Federal Government, which caused death, starvation and huger in

---

[5]Lewis, J. 2007

[6]*"Los relatos breves de Chinua Achebe entroncan indudablemente con la secular tradición cuentística de su etnia, lo cual [...] se refiere a su valor didáctico"* (García P. 1998, p. 418)

a faster way by the use of bombs and army. We move from hope towards disillusionment, from innocence towards pain. The weakest characters died at the end and those who acted corruptly some time ago such as Reginald remain alive but will have to cope with their worst punishment: keeping on living after a war, keeping on leaving quiet tradition and facing a violent modernity.

On the other hand, we have Ngugi Wa Thiong'o's short story "A Meeting in the Dark", which is set in a Kikuyu community in Kenya. So now we move to East Africa. There is an easily recognizable dichotomy in the names of the characters: John and his family with Western names versus his lover, Wamuhu with traditional Kikuyu names. We have to consider that the author himself found this controversy of identity by means of changing his Western name: James to the traditional African one of Ngugi. Names hide very much symbolism as far as identity and culture are concerned.

As we found in Chinua Achebe's "Girls at War", we have a conflict in the encounter between the new ways of seeing reality coming from the colonizer and the old traditional rules of African communities. Nevertheless, this encounter and lack of identity is stronger and better represented in this short story because its illocutionary force and intention are also different. Ngugui wants us to reflect on the value of our community and the importance of feeling accepted, the influence it has on our construction of identity.

John is our main character and he is the son of Stanley, who converted into Christianity, the religion of the colonizer because he got his mother Susana pregnant of him before getting married and this was a violation on the values of the community. This is an example of "Acculturation", that is, the process of accepting the Western culture and religion on the part of a tribe. John will be from his birth immersed in a religion which he did not feel as his original one. He missed those traditional fairy tales of the tribe his mother Susana (who represents tradition) used to tell him in order to understand his reality: *"His mother had stopped telling him stories long ago"* (p. 71) because his father (modernity), following Western values, prohibited it: "Then the white men had come, preaching a strange religion, strange ways, which all men followed. The tribe's code of behavior was broken".

John misses the life of a tribe he does not belong to anymore: *"They were obviously enjoying themselves. They are more free than I am. He envied their exuberance. They clearly stood outside or above the strict morality that the educated ones had to be judged by"* (p. 75). So this contact with Western culture makes him feel trapped too. He has an in-between feeling of displacement. He feels not belonging anywhere. This is a result of the clash between the culture of his environment (traditional African one, which was not really his) and Western Calvinist culture (which was official his but did not feel like belonging to it).

This has to do with the initial symbolic story which appears as a flashback of Susana telling it to John many years ago: The stranger which appears in the story represents the colonizer giving Africans new opportunities by means of Western education. They are encouraged to convert into a new religion and travel abroad to the metropolis in order to get university education. That is what the metaphor of going further "the hill" means: *"Then one day a stranger came [...] Then, he told them a beautiful country beyond the hill"* (p. 68).

There is another change in this included tale: now the colonizer becomes an Irimu, an ogre and this symbolizes how colonizers led the community to a sense of displacement in which it was impossible to feel neither from Africa nor from the metropolis: *"She had no home to go and she could not look forward to the beautiful land, to see all the good things, because the Irimu was in the way"* (p. 68). This "Irimu in the way" represents the concept of displacement and paralysis because of clash of identities. Some Africans like John feel like not belonging to anywhere and as a result have a feeling of isolation and incomprehensibility on the part of society.

But his situation goes even worse when he lives the same his father did with his mother: he meets an African traditional girl, and leaves her pregnant. The conflict between what seems to be "love for a girl from tradition" and "ambition for being accepted" by his Westernized father clashes again. As Wamuhu is circumcised, he knows that his Christian father would not accept her and all his future studying abroad would be lost: *"The men who followed the new faith would not let the girls be circumcised. And they would not let their sons marry circumcised girls"* (p. 76).

The importance of dreams is also a reflection of the traditional meaning the tribe gave on them, as powerful foreseers of the future: *"Dreams about circumcision were not good. They portended death"* (p. 80). He feels disoriented, unable of reveling against his father, his Western side. This disorientation leads him to anxiety and from anxiety to madness. The only solution he found was destruction and the author relates it to the violent way of behavior on the part of the colonizer.

Conclusion

To conclude, in the end this clash of identities added to the rejection on the part of Wamuhu to hide him as father of their future child, makes him go insane and kills her. He acts like the colonizer, who arrives into a land, builds there and then destroys it. He does just the same, invades a female body (which is related to the land as symbol of fertility) and then kills it, being a member of his own community. Nonetheless, just to mention Bessie Head's "The Prisoner Who Wore Glasses", even though it was not an issue in this essay, we have to consider that here the roles of white and black men are inverted and this is quite ironical. In a sense, we find this same inversion in a constant clash of identities in this short story by means of the unique figure of John.

Both short stories have a dramatic tone and end in death, destruction and disillusionment. There are open endings in both of them and this makes us think that both Ngugui's John as Achebe's Reginald are going to live in isolation after experiencing a conflict: a national one in "Girls at War" and a personal one in "A Meeting in the Dark" which will lead them to displacement in a constant, dangerous clash between humanity and evilness, between corruption and solidarity, between tradition and modernity.

REFERENCES

A) Electronic sources:

-Lewis, J. "Noble Savage", *A Guide to the Political Left*. 30th January 2007. Accessed on 5th Nov. 2014. http://www.discoverthenetworks.org/viewSubCategory.asp?id=720

-Charles E. "Style and Technique" *Comprehensive Guide to Short Stories, Critical Edition*. 2004. Accessed on 7th Nov. 2014, http://www.enotes.com/topics/meeting-dark/in-depth#in-depth-style-and-technique

-Brendon, N. *Ngugi Wa Thiong'o Gender and the Ethics of Postcolonial Reading*. Ashgat Publishing Ltd, Surrey, 2010. ProQuest ebrary.web. Electronic book. Acessed on 6th Nov. 2014

B) Books:

-Booker, K. *The Chinua Achebe Encyclopedia*. Greenwood Press. The United States of America. 2003.

-García P. *La Narrativa Nigeriana en Lengua Inglesa: Chinua Achebe o el Reverso de la Utopía*. Capítulo II: "La Narrativa de Chinua Achebe". Tesis Doctoral. Universidad de Granada. 1998.

-Ashcroft, B. *The Empire Writes Back*. Taylor & Francis Group. London. 1989